As Kingfishers Catch Fire

As kingfishers catch fire, dragonflies draw flame;
As tumbled over rim in roundy wells
Stones ring; like each tucked string tells, each hung bell's
Bow swung finds tongue to fling out broad its name;
Each mortal thing does one thing and the same:
Deals out that being indoors each one dwells;
Selves — goes itself; *myself* it speaks and spells,
Crying *What I do is me: for that I came.*

I say more: the just man justices;
Keeps grace: that keeps all his goings graces;
Acts in God's eye what in God's eye he is —
Christ — for Christ plays in ten thousand places,
Lovely in limbs, and lovely in eyes not his
To the Father through the features of men's faces.

Gerard Manley Hopkins

Dedication

In memory of my dad
Jim Hamilton
(15 July 1931–28 January 2009)

On the day before he died, he made a mysterious prophecy about a foreign country. He spoke of Holy Spirit hospitals for the healing of land and people in the tiny towns along the East Coast of New Zealand. For many years, I forgot about his words — never expecting they could possibly be fulfilled.

But then the day came when an unexpected email popped into my inbox. As it did, the Holy Spirit whispered to my heart that it was about that last prophecy of my dad's. It took two whole days for my mind to calm sufficiently to open the message.

And, when I did, my breath was taken away by some of the exact phrases my dad had used.

The message, of course, came from a tiny town in New Zealand.

So this book is dedicated to the many people from around the world who have been quietly drawn there to pray into the land. It is especially dedicated to Joy and Richard, as well as Desiree and Waipatu, who are pioneering the healing of history in one of those tiny East Coast towns.

May you all be blessed with His kiss as you work with Him to bring this bent world back into alignment.

Exceptional thanks to my mother, Dell, for writing the uplifting prayers; to Genevieve for the beautiful paintings; and to Rebekah for the gorgeous design.

Anne Hamilton
Seventeen MIle Rocks, 2020

Contents

1	*As Kingfishers Catch Fire*
5	Introduction
6	*Caesarea Philippi*
8	**Piper at the Gates**
24	Caesarea Philippi: the Roman and Greek past
27	Caesarea Philippi: the tribal past
28	Caesarea Philippi: the primeval past
29	Caesarea Philippi: the near future
30	Celebrating the Day
33	Prayer
34	The Meaning of Hermon
35	Discussion Questions
38	*Mount Hermon*
40	**Weight of Glory**
56	Notes about the healing of Mt. Hermon's history
61	Prayer
64	Discussion Questions
64	Coda
67	Accepting Jesus as the Messiah
68	Acknowledgments and Attributions
70	*God's Grandeur*

BENT WORLD, Bright Wings

Introduction

When I'm travelling, I like to linger in places. Instead of a rush of varied experiences, I prefer to savour the atmosphere in just a few localities. I want to get a feel for what the people of ancient Rome called the 'genius loci', *the spirit of a place.*

Several years ago I was in the lowlands of Scotland. It took me seventeen days before I was finally able to crystallise its sense of 'place' in my mind. 'This,' I said to myself, 'is not just a landscape that has been criss-crossed by hundreds of armies, it's a landscape that breeds armies.'

As soon as I thought that, I looked up the oldest name on record for the area. It went back over two thousand years to a Caledonian tribe known as the Gadeni, *men of battle*. Even today, the landscape still resonates strongly with ancient names indicating their presence long ago. And perhaps it is no coincidence that 'gad' is a Hebrew word for *troops* as well as *fortune*.

In the first book in this series, *Like Wildflowers, Suddenly,* 'gad' is highlighted in a series of healings that Jesus performed. He was always very intentional about the way He addressed the wounds of history — not just for people but also for places. In each locality, His actions were attuned to the very deepest pain tormenting the land.

This second book, *Bent World, Bright Wings,* continues to highlight the actions of Jesus in transforming the lament of the land into a song of praise for its Creator. As previously, there's a mix of narrative and non-fiction — intended to put you in the scene itself and bring you insight into the cultural nuances at the time. It also contains prayers and discussion questions. It might be an unusual mix for a book but it's intended to have an internal geography that is healing in itself. And, on occasion, it works — as Jenny testifies here about *Like Wildflowers, Suddenly*:

> My 15 year old daughter read it and said, 'It made me realise that when Jesus said confusing things, there was actually so much more to what He was doing and saying than meets the eye.'
>
> And the power and truth in the prayers is indescribable. As I prayed one of them aloud, coupled with the insight the stories had given me, I know something changed, not just deep inside me but in the situation in my life that had been crippling me spiritually. God whispered truth, discernment and peace into my soul.

Bent World, Bright Wings is another overture in words and pictures to the way Jesus healed history. It's a much richer, denser tapestry than the previous volume — so, in many ways, it's not a light read. But it's breathtaking to see how Jesus binds up the complex fractures of the past in so few words. His actions are economical, efficient, elegant.

And they all involve restoring the *shalom* of 'place'. .

Anne Hamilton
Seventeen Mile Rocks, 2020

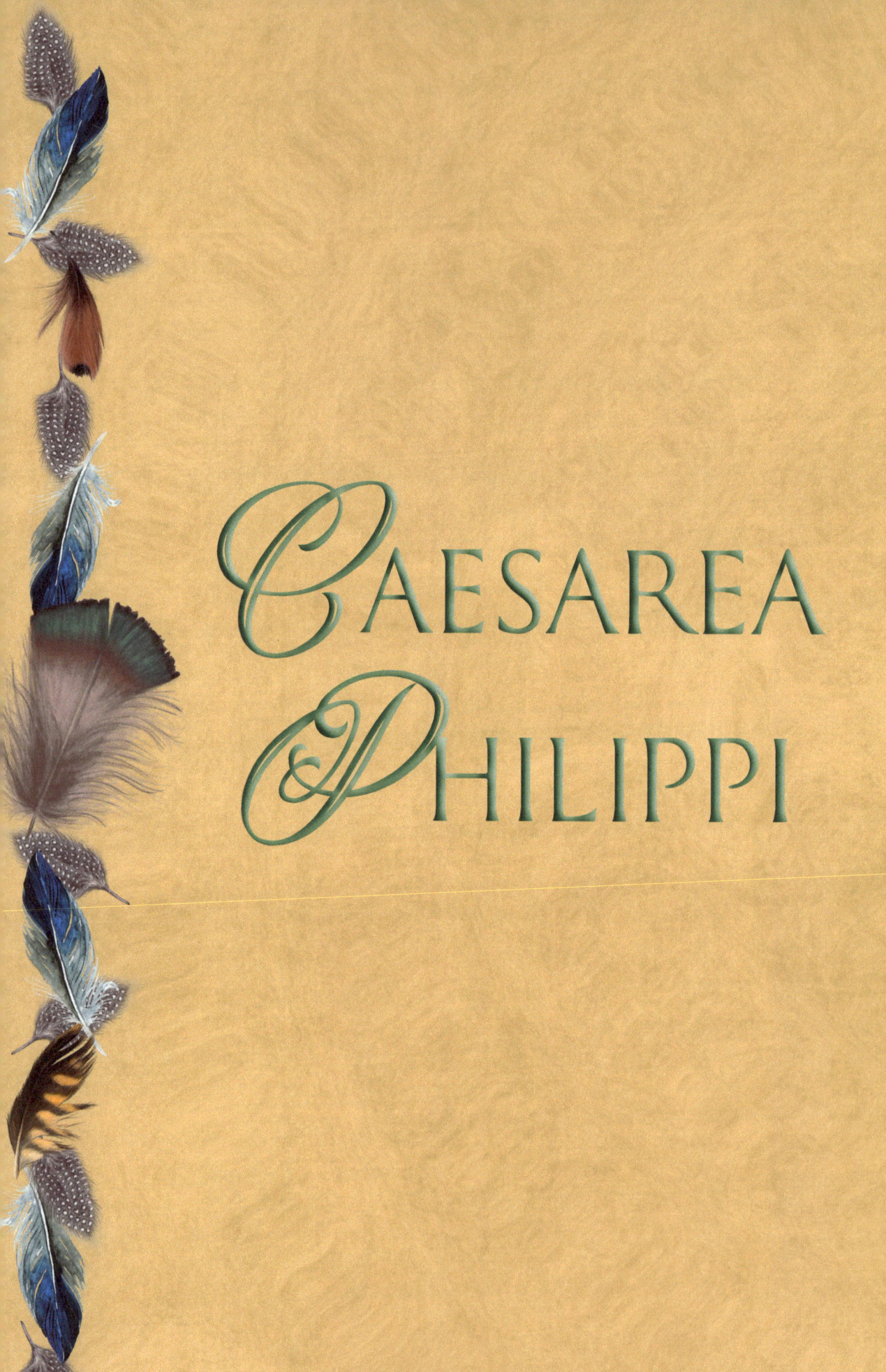

Caesarea & Philippi

And I also say to you that you are Peter,
and on this rock I will build My church,
and the gates of Hades shall not prevail against it.

Matthew 16:18 NKJ

Acts 9:3 ISV

As Saul travelled along and was approaching Damascus,
a light from Heaven suddenly flashed around him.

'Lord ... here are two swords.'
'That is enough!'
He told them.
Luke 22:38 HCSB

Piper at the Gates

This is a fictional account — I wanted this story to come from the perspective of an 'outsider' with sufficient knowledge of sacred ritual to understand the significance of Jesus' words and actions. Hence the choice of Malchus who is mentioned twice in the gospel of John.

My name is Malchus. A strange name, I know, for a slave. My father thought that, if he called me *king*, he'd forge a new destiny for me. That eventually I'd escape servitude and break free of our family's ancestral ties to the household of the high priest. The master could have overruled, of course, but I think it amused him to have a 'king' as his servant.

These days no one calls me Malchus.[1] 'One Ear' is what they've dubbed me, even though I have two quite serviceable ones. The name has stuck because of that strange incident with Simon in the garden the night Jesus was arrested.[2]

1 & 2.
John 18:10

Simon, you probably know, lashed out with his sword. And took off my ear. And Jesus put it back on.

But my connection with Jesus began long before that fateful night. It started, months before, at the Feast of Trumpets. As you probably know, the New Year cannot officially be announced with a blast from a shofar until the new moon is sighted.[3] So there I was with Caiaphas — yes, the high priest himself — on the rooftop on an evening that was blustery, overcast and unseasonably cold. No sign whatsoever of the moon. Caiaphas was quickly tired of waiting around and shivering with a runny, snuffly nose. So he handed the shofar to me and instructed me to stay there until moonset, if need be, and blow it the moment I caught sight of the new moon. *This*, I thought to myself, *is definitely not kosher. It's the duty of a priest, not of a priest's slave.*

3.
Rosh Hashanah, the Feast of Trumpets, is the first day of the Jewish New Year. Strictly speaking, it cannot be officially declared until the new moon is sighted, at which time a shofar blast is sounded. It occurs during the early autumn of the Northern Hemisphere.

Still as you can guess, I said nothing. Caiaphas was barely gone two minutes when the clouds parted and the moon appeared: a faint golden sliver just above the western horizon. I hesitated as I raised the shofar to my lips. *Should I call Caiaphas back? What if he got here and the clouds had closed over once more?* So I just turned off my fear of God and blew. It was a croaky wobble at first because I'd never done anything like it before but then a full-throated roar broke forth.

I stopped, bowed to heaven, and fled from the rooftop. I was putting the shofar away when Caiaphas slammed down a bag of money next to me. 'Go and join the disciples of Jesus.'

'My Lord Caiaphas!' I knew he had spies amongst the outer seventy of the Galilean's followers and perhaps even in the inner twelve. Whispers had come back about Nicodemus[4] and Joseph of Arimathea[5] — yet he knew that to accuse such wealthy, influential men without proof could backfire seriously.

Caiaphas flicked the leather thong of the money bag towards me. 'It's exactly ten days to Yom Kippur. If Jesus is to proclaim himself as the Messiah, it's the logical time. The logical place is here in Jerusalem — when the crowds gather at the Temple. We need to stop him before that happens — before the Romans see the need to intervene.'

'So you need to know his plans beforehand.' My mind was racing. *What has happened to the watchers? Have they all defected and joined the Jesus movement? Or... are they sending conflicting reports? And he doesn't know which one of them to trust?*

Well, long story short, I took the money bag and set off north. I knew what Caiaphas expected — he wanted to dispel the rumours one way or another and he knew I'd be able to recognise anyone from the Sanhedrin secretly meeting with the Galilean rabbi. He also wanted advance warning of any move by Jesus to restore the kingship of David's line. Everyone had been predicting *that* since the beginning of summer.

It took me three and a half days to reach Capernaum and, wherever I stopped, the news was always buzzing with stories about Jesus that

4.
John 3:1–15; John 7:50 and John 19:39

5.
John 19:38

'I am a rose of Sharon...'
Song of Songs 1:17 NIV

I am overshadowed by God's love,
armoured by a song in the gate.

defied logic and credibility. He'd turned water into wine! He'd fed five thousand men with just five loaves and two fish! He'd cast a legion of demons out of a man! He'd given sight to a man born blind! He'd walked on water!

Sure! As if! That was the thought behind my careful smile back then. The trouble was that the people relating the stories seemed sensible and level-headed. They were hard-nosed, not fluffy-minded. Several claimed to have seen one of the miracles with their own eyes. And they claimed they were not alone. One shifty-eyed innkeeper insisted that the wife of King Herod's steward[6] was *the* big financial backer who made the entire Jesus roadshow possible. I wondered if Caiaphas had heard that particular rumour. I knew Joanna, and I knew Herod's manager Chuza.[7] I couldn't see him risking his position through such an unsavoury connection.

6.
Luke 8:3 and Luke 24:10

I thought it would be hard to join the followers of Jesus but he wasn't like other rabbis. It was just a matter of moving along with the ebb and flow of humanity swirling around him. It was easy to strike up conversation by sharing a basket of bread or a flagon of wine. In the first afternoon, I'd joked around with Justus[8] and got acquainted with Matthias[9]. I thought they were on the edge but I quickly found

'...a holy convocation announced with blasts on the *shofar*.'
Leviticus 23:24 CJB

7.
Luke 8:3 and perhaps also Romans 16:7. It is sometimes suggested that the woman named Junia whom Paul describes as an apostle and who was 'in the Lord before' he was is actually Joanna. This is because the Hebrew equivalent to the Latin name 'Junia' is 'Joanna'. She may also be related to Paul.

8.
Acts 1:23, also called Joseph and Barsabbas

9.
Acts 1:23

they'd been with Jesus from the days of John the Baptist. They were both thick with Matthew who regaled us with stories from his days as a tax collector.[10] I soon realised he was one of the inner twelve. And just as quickly I picked up that the ones closest to Jesus had no more clue of what he was planning than Caiaphas did. They didn't even know where he was. 'Up some mountain, praying,' was Matthew's response to my casually posed question.

'...take the first fish...and ...you will find a shekel...'
Matthew 17:27 ESV

'You sure?' Justus asked.

'Of course I'm sure.' Matthew's shrug was off-hand. 'Do you see crowds rushing anywhere? Do you hear a hubbub in the distance? Do you smell burning stew because half the neighbourhood has abandoned dinner preparation to chase him?' He winked at Justus. 'The moment someone spots him, we'll know he's arrived by these signs.'

10. Matthew 9:9

11. John 13:29

12. Matthew 17:27

I thought of the frenzied detail that the household steward impressed on us when threatened by even the slightest change in routine for Caiaphas. And I wondered if the disciples of Jesus were always prepared for his return. Or never prepared.

Nightfall came and there was no sign of him. I found that Matthew was the scribe of the twelve. He'd collected the parables Jesus told and was more than willing to read them over a platter of figs and dates, grapes and pomegranates. It was such a companionable evening I began to hate deceiving them all.

The next day was more of the same. No sign of Jesus. I wandered down by the lake, meeting with Justus and Matthew once more. Matthias had gone in search of their fellowship's treasurer, Judas, to take some money from the common purse.[11] That seemed to be a cue for Matthew to launch into a story about Jesus not having money for the temple tax and sending Simon out fishing. The first fish he caught had the silver coin for the tax in its mouth.[12]

I felt a chill run up my spine as he laughed, oblivious to the nuances of the tale. 'Don't you understand?' I asked. 'It's the temple shekel. From the mint in Tyre. It's got a picture of Hercules Melkart on it.'[13]

I stared at him. *How could a tax collector have missed something so obvious?* I spelled it out for him. I knew this. Knew it from the fear freezing my bones. Melkart: *king of the city,* a meaning so close to my own name that, when I was a child, I'd always felt my hair stand on end when he was mentioned. 'Melkart — the king of Tyre. The Scriptures call him Moloch — godling of death. The one who demanded the sacrifice of the firsborn in the bronze hands of fire.' I took a deep breath to calm my racing heart. 'The fish Simon caught spat out Death itself.'

'Just as a fish once spat out Jonah.'[14] Justus raised a hand. His eyes gleamed.

I nodded. 'The sign of Jonah.' I had no idea then of the prophecy in my words. This was many months before Jesus was to throw the money-changers out of the Temple,[15] clearing out the same silver shekels with the god of Death and his blasphemous motto blazoned

13.
In the time of Jesus, the Jewish people were not permitted by their Roman overlords to mint their own coins. There were several options available to them — however, the highest quality silver came from the mint at Tyre with the words 'Tyre holy and inviolable' on it (as shown below) and a picture of Hercules Melkart, who was the equivalent of Moloch, the god of death and child sacrifice. The temple hierarchy selected these coins, rather than inferior silver with their own choice of images on it.

14.
Jonah 2:10

15.
Matthew 21:12

on them, an action entirely prophetic of the day he cast Death out of his tomb.

I was in. My impassioned speech had convinced them all I was a true believer. We spent the rest of the day together, eating and drinking and story-telling. I was introduced to the fishermen, Simon and his brother Andrew along with their friend John. There was an awkward moment when John looked at me quizzically, as if he recognised me. I certainly recognised him. He'd paid regular visits over the years to some of his family who served in the high priest's household.[16] But they were not bond-slaves like my brothers and cousins. Family loyalty was the reason Caiaphas trusted me with this mission: he knew I would do all I could to protect my own.

But John said nothing. So neither did I.

Night fell but Jesus still didn't come. The fishermen in the group decided that, although the moon was just a quarter crescent, the skies were clear and it would be a good evening for taking out the boat. Matthew was happy enough to leave them to it and wait with me by the shore. We kindled a tiny fire and I listened to his endless supply of stories about Jesus casting demons out of people. But, as one tale followed another, I realised Jesus was also casting demons out of the land. I fell asleep to the lapping of waves on the shore.

Dawn came and, with it, the boat. Andrew and John were just pulling in to shore when Jesus just appeared and strolled along the shoreline. Without a word, he slipped aboard. He pointed east and the boat took off once again, gliding into the sunrise.

No one seemed disconcerted by this mysterious behaviour. We simply set off, walking around the lake. Around midday we caught up with them. By that time, the seventy had straggled in after us. It would be cutting it fine by my calculations, but a brisk journey south along the old King's Highway[17] should bring us to Jerusalem just in time for Yom Kippur.

16.
John 18:16 refers to an anonymous disciple who knew the high priest. It is generally considered this is the writer, John.

17.
Numbers 21:22

18.
Deuteronomy 3:11

'Jesus went... to the villages of Caesarea Philippi...'
Mark 8:27 ESV

So I was puzzled when Jesus began to head in the opposite direction. North. Into the wilderness of the old darkness. Towards the ancient land of Bashan — the territory of Og, the last of the ghostly Rephaim, whose massive iron bed was nine cubits long and four cubits wide.[18] Yes, exactly the same size as the ritual marriage bed of Marduk, the bull-calf of the fifty names, the patron deity of Babylon.[19] Indeed, we were soon traversing the haunted landscape of the bulls of Bashan, where once the giants descended from the fallen angels had had their stronghold.[20]

By the end of the day I realised we weren't going to turn around. And I was beginning to wonder if I should. It wasn't as if I feared going into the serpent's realm,[21] it was simply that it wasn't as easy leaving the followers of Jesus as it had been joining. I couldn't sneak off undetected. Out there, far from anywhere, everyone was watching out for each other, making sure food was available, sharing water freely, practising prayers that followed the model explained by Jesus. After I got over the shock of calling God 'Abba', *Daddy*,[22] I warmed to it with an enthusiasm I found almost reckless.

So, long story short again, I stayed — all the way up into the foothills of Hermon, the very snow-capped mountain where the fallen angels descended and pledged themselves to pursue the daughters of humanity. The sun was just dipping below the horizon when we set up camp not far from the old sanctuary of apostate Dan. I was still

19.
Michael Heiser, *The Unseen Realm,* Lexham Press 2015

20.
Michael Heiser, *The Unseen Realm,* Lexham Press 2015

21.
Michael Heiser in *The Unseen Realm* relates the word 'bashan' to *serpent*.

22.
Mark 14:36

Gladiators were called *barley men* because of their diet of grains and pulses. The Hebrew for *barley* and *goat* both derive from the word for *hairy*.

23.
2 Chronicles 11:15 refers to the golden calf idols that Jeroboam set up, as well goat-demons.

24.
Matthew 14:8

25.
Cleopatra is usually said to mean *glory of the fatherland*, however it can also mean *keys of the fatherland*.

thinking of bulls and ghosts, and half-expected to see a shadowy image of the golden calf that had once been worshipped there.²³

Yom Kippur, the Day of Atonement, was just beginning. As I sat by a fire that evening and watched Jesus through the showering sparks, I scanned the company, trying to work out which of them were in the pay of Caiaphas. I came to no conclusions. Jesus was fingering the knots on the fringe of his shawl. I realised that, even here, in the midst of us all, he was praying in silence.

Philip seemed to know the history of the region — he apparently had a natural curiosity due to the fact it was ruled by his namesake, Philip the Tetrarch. Yes, the same Philip who was the half-brother of Herod, but not the same half-brother who'd been married to Herodias. She was the one who divorced one brother to marry another and who asked for the head of John the Baptist on a platter.²⁴

He regaled us with an impression of how Cleopatra had received this territory last century as a gift from her lover Mark Antony. The waggle of his eyebrows and batting of eyelashes completely ruined the severity of his regal sideways hand pose. We all laughed at his Egyptian impersonations as he went on about Pharaoh Cleo's penchant for living up to her name as the key to the fatherland.²⁵

She was certainly able to unlock any number of hostile barriers when it came to Roman generals — even peacock-hearted Julius Caesar had acknowledged the son she bore to him.[26] And of course there was the rumour that had never gone away — that she was in fact the mother of Philip the Tetrarch. His mother was definitely named Cleopatra[27] but whether she was the same as the infamous Queen of the Nile is an open question. Maybe the confusion came about because Cleopatra's Guard came into the employ of Herod the Great on her death.[28] Of course, people still say that old Herod feared her territorial ambitions far too much to have had an intimate liaison with her — but the great fox was well known for his cunning in keeping his friends close and his enemies closer.

I thought at one point during the laughter that Jesus was going to come over and put a stop to the antics. It wasn't the most edifying conversation for the start of the Day of Atonement. But he just looked at us — *at me*, I thought — and said nothing. I felt torn. The pressure to flee was intense, the pressure to remain equally so. I had to go. I just needed an opportunity to get away, undetected.

26.
Caesarion, the last Pharaoh. Officially Ptolemy XV Philopator Philometor Caesar.

27.
Philip's mother is known to be Cleopatra of Jerusalem. History records nothing about her except her name. Speculation that she was actually Cleopatra of Egypt cannot be verified on the one hand or totally discounted on the other. Philip is thought to have been born a few years after her death — however since the date of his birth is uncertain, the possibility that she is his mother cannot be entirely ruled out.

28.
Four hundred Galatians who formed Cleopatra's personal bodyguard entered the service of Herod the Great on her death. These Celtic mercenaries then went on to figure prominently in Herod's funeral service.

'...a goat with a prominent horn ... came from the west, crossing the whole earth'

Daniel 8:5 NIV

'Who do you say I am?'
Matthew 16:15 BSB

29.
Matthew 16:13

It didn't come that night. And early in the morning we were up and off. Jesus rounded us up and led us into Caesarea Philippi.[29] There are dozens of temples dotted around the town but he headed straight for the most notorious of all: the shrine to Pan the piper.[30] I don't consider myself the most spiritually sensitive of men but even I could feel the oppression there. I wasn't surprised at the fear — Pan is, after all, the lord of panic — but the horror was palpable.[31] Was Jesus going to take us right up to the Gates of Hades — the place where sacrificial victims were fed a numbing narcotic and then thrown into the tunnel of death where rushing waters would hurtle them down to the underworld?

Thankfully he stopped and faced the pool in front of the shrine. I admit that, at that moment, I began to wonder about his sanity. What on earth was a rabbi so many Jews hoped was the Messiah doing at the shrine of a half-goat half-human godling like Pan?

30.
Pan pipes or the pan flute is a musical instrument made of hollow reeds of different lengths bound together. The pipes are named after Pan, the Greek godling of nature and shepherds who was often depicted with such an instrument. When Jesus calls Himself 'the Good Shepherd', He is claiming back for God a title usurped by Pan.

I took a deep breath. What a vile, defiled place to come to on Yom Kippur. At this moment, Caiaphas would be entering beyond the veil into the Holy of Holies with his censer of incense. He would already have offered a bull in atonement for his own sins and that of his household. I felt a sense of relief at that, knowing I was included. He would be about to sprinkle the blood seven times in front of the mercy-seat covering the Ark of the Covenant.

And then it hit me. He would also have already cast the lots over the goats for the sin offering: one to be sacrificed to the Lord and the other — the scapegoat — to be sent into the wilderness. *Goat. Wilderness. Sacrifice.*

Goat: Pan. *Wilderness*: Bashan. *Sacrifice*: Gates of Hell.

31.
The word 'panic' derives from the name of the goat-man, Pan.

'You are the Christ...'
Matthew 16:16 BSB

The symbolism was too exact. I looked around the disciples in dismay. Which one of them was the scapegoat?

Jesus turned. I'll never forget what he said next. 'Who do people say that the Son of Man is?'[32] It was a question for his disciples. But I thought he was looking at me as he asked. I later found that everyone there that day thought he'd been staring at them.

There was a moment's hesitation. Then: 'John the Baptist, returned from the dead.'

And: 'Elijah.'

'Jeremiah.'

'One of the prophets.'[33]

'But who do you say that I am?'[34]

Again the hesitation. Then Simon spoke. 'You are the Messiah, the Son of the living God.'[35]

Jesus nodded. 'Blessed are you, Simon son of Jonah! For flesh and blood has not revealed this truth to you. It comes from my heavenly Father. I tell you, you are Cephas, and on this cornerstone I will build my church, and the gates of hell shall not prevail against it. I will give

'On this rock I will build My church...'
Matthew 16:17–18 BSB

32. Matthew 16:13

33. Matthew 16:14

34. Matthew 16:15

35. Matthew 16:16

you the keys of the kingdom of heaven, and whatever you bind on earth shall be bound in heaven, and whatever you loose on earth shall be loosed in heaven.'36

Today, as I look back on those words, I see what I missed at the time: their embedded weight of glory. When you're part of the high priest's household, it's important to be fluent in several languages — not simply to converse with guests, but sometimes to spy on them. To me, those words make sense across more than one tongue.

Dense and rich with impartation, they were the hinge opening a new age. For a moment, it was as the veil of time was ripped and I was there, amongst the countless swirling stars as God said to Abram, 'I am El Shaddai; walk before Me and be blameless.'37 As the father of our nation fell facedown, the Lord Almighty continued, 'No longer shall your name be called Abram, but your name shall be Abraham.'38

It was a renaming to begin a new kingdom, just as the renaming of Abraham led to a new nation. *Cephas*, that's what Jesus called Simon. It was essentially the same name as that of my master, the high priest Caiaphas. In an instant, I knew that Jesus was the scapegoat who had been driven into the wilderness. And I knew that Caiaphas had missed more than his chance: he'd missed his true calling. At this very moment, in Jerusalem, Caiaphas should have proclaimed Jesus as the Messiah — but he had failed. His place had been given to another: the bumptious, bucolic, impetuous fisherman Simon.

The renaming was covenantal in form, just like that of Abraham. There had been the exchange of names — 'Messiah, Son of the living God' was given to Jesus by Simon. In return he'd received Cephas, *cornerstone*. During an exchange of names, you can only give what is your own, so in that moment Jesus asserted his right to the title of Chief Cornerstone from the scroll of the prophet Isaiah.39

I look back now, reflecting on all the landscape we'd traversed and I realise how simply its healing had been accomplished. Jesus had merely spoken to it. As once the Lord God had spoken the world in being, so Jesus spoke it into healing.

36.
Matthew 16:17–19
Emphasis added as follows: the usual translation of *rock* has been altered to *cornerstone* in this verse to reflect the nuances of Cephas in Hebrew wording. Cephas is not simply *rock* but refers to the *threshold stone* under the entrance to a house. This stone underneath the door is the *cornerstone*.

37.
Genesis 17:1

38.
Genesis 17:5

39.
Isaiah 28:16

Notes

Let's now examine in some detail the words of Jesus that imparted healing to the land. There are many facets to His words and bitter theological wars have raged over them. But the focus of this reflection is on an overlooked aspect: how His words are divinely crafted to speak deep into history.

His declaration has nuances that cover the Roman past, the Greek past, the tribal past, the primeval past and even the near future. Despite its brevity, it also manages to encompass geography, current events and contemporary personalities, as well as celebrate the date of the declaration itself.

The Roman Past

In the century prior to the visit of Jesus, this region had been the property of Cleopatra, queen of Egypt. She had been given the territory by her lover, Mark Antony, who had had the previous ruler executed for supporting the Persians against the Romans. Her name meant *glory of the father* or *keys of the fatherland*. Jesus masterfully puns on this with His words, *keys of the kingdom*. In doing so, He speaks as the prophets so often did: in wordplay and poetry.

The Greek Past

Before the time of Cleopatra, a temple precinct dedicated to the rustic deity Pan[40] had been set up after Israel was conquered by Alexander the Great. In the vision of the prophet Daniel which reveals the destruction of the Persian empire by that of Alexander's Greek armies, the Persians are symbolised by a ram and the Greeks by a goat.[41] Pan was half-human, half-goat.[42] From his ability to rout opposing troops, sending them fleeing in terror because of his ghastly shriek, comes the word *panic*.

40.
Caesarea Philippi: Banias, the Lost City of Pan, John Francis Wilson, I.B. Tauris, 2004

41.
Daniel 8:21

42.
A stark contrast to Jesus as fully human, fully divine.

'...the gates of Hades will not prevail...'
Matthew 16:18 BSB

The Greek cultic shrine dedicated to him included a cave with gushing spring.[43] Here, so it was said, were the very 'Gates of Hades' and into this cave, sacrificial offerings — including bound and drugged humans — were thrown.

When Jesus speaks of the 'Gates of Hades' He was almost certainly standing right in front of them — and when He says they will not prevail against His church, He is speaking on several levels. Even the greatest conqueror, in human terms, of the known world could not defeat His beloved. The powers of the underworld — Hades[44] and the spirits of the dead — could not triumph over His bride. The spirit of panic — Pan, *lord of the sources*,[45] could not overthrow His betrothed.

Perhaps for our own times, there is a message: even the philosophy of the Greeks which has so pervaded the church Jesus loves will ultimately bow before Him.

The Hebrew for *barley*, *goat*, *satyr*, *devil* and *hairy* are related.

43.
Because of an earthquake, the water now seeps from the bedrock below.

44.
The name Hades means *unseen* or *not idol*.

45.
In *Caesarea Philippi: Banias, the Lost City of Pan*, John Francis Wilson equates Pan with Aliyan, one of the Baals of the Canaanites, who was considered *lord of the springs* or *lord of the sources*.

THE TRIBAL PAST

Paneas, the temple of Pan, was often mistaken in ancient writings for the sanctuary of the tribe of Dan. Archaeological digs, however, locate Dan about six kilometres away. The sanctuary at Dan was a pilgrimage site set up in opposition to the temple in Jerusalem. Not only did a rival monarchy exist, due to a split in the kingdom when ten tribes rebelled against the house of David, but so did a competing priesthood.

The descendants of two of the most famous brothers in Israelite history — Moses and Aaron — became adversaries for the position of high priest.[46] In Jerusalem the high priests came from the line of Aaron. However in Dan, where the worship of golden calves and goat-demons[47] came to be prominent, the high priests came from the line of Moses.

The name Dan means *judge*. In the tribal past, there were no kings to govern the land. Instead the judges sat at the city gates to dispense their verdicts. In fact, 'gates' and judges were synonymous. So when Jesus refers to the 'Gates of Hades', it could be a double entendre, also referring to the sanctuary at Dan.[48] After all, goat-demons were worshipped at Dan and the goat-man Pan was worshipped at the Paneion. Both places would have a resonance evocative of *judges of the underworld*.

The idea of judgment is reinforced by Jesus' subsequent words about *binding* and *loosing*. These are terms that refer to legal injunctions — 'deó', *bind* meaning *to declare unlawful* or *to prohibit*, while 'luó', *loose* means *to annul, to release, to break, to contravene* or *to discharge from prison*.[49]

46.
Perhaps the long shadow of the hostility between Cain and Abel or Jacob and Esau played out in this generations-long rivalry which seems to have started with the grandsons of both Aaron and Moses.

47.
The Day of Atonement was originally set up to stop the sacrifices by some Israelites to goat-demons. (Leviticus 17:7) However, the worship of the goat-demons as well as the golden calves was re-instated under Jeroboam, first king of Israel. (2 Chronicles 11:15)

48.
In fact, it might well be a triple entendre — since one of the words for *goat* in Hebrew has identical spelling to a word for *gate*.

49.
These words, *binding* and *loosing*, are also used outside a legal context for *tying up* and of course for *untying* respectively. However, given that Jesus was setting up His governmental assembly, the legal interpretation seems most likely. Jesus calls His church 'ekklésia' — which, as Derek Prince points out in *Rediscovering God's Church* is 'knesset' in Hebrew, the same word as is used for the Israeli parliament.

THE PRIMEVAL PAST

Beginning in the days of Jared, the great-great-great grandson of Adam, the angelic sons of God descended from the heavens and took wives for themselves from amongst the daughters of men.[50] Their children were giants — the nephilim — who became the heroes of old.[51] The book of Enoch, although quoted extensively by the gospel and epistle writers, is not considered part of the canon of Scripture. However it says that the location where these fallen angels — the Watchers — came to earth was Mount Hermon, looming high above Caesarea Philippi on its south-western slopes.

Here they threw curses at one another: their action giving rise to one of the meanings of Hermon — *accursed*.[52] The leader of the angelic cohort was apparently concerned that those with him would not follow through with their plan to marry the most beautiful of the human women. He was suspicious he'd be left to take the responsibility and the punishment alone. To bind them into adhering to their agreement, he extracted vows from them and, to seal the matter, they had then pronounced curses over each other regarding the breaking of those vows.

The echoes of this diabolic agreement are found in the words of Jesus as He sets in place the means of overturning it: 'Whatever you *bind* on earth shall be bound in heaven, and whatever you *loose* on earth shall be loosed in heaven.' Here is the prophecy that the church will triumph over all the schemes of the evil one to corrupt humanity, that the government He is setting up will have the power to nullify any conspiracy conceived by hell.

For here, as His words couple with the creative power of the One who spoke the heavens and earth into being, is the moment when the church was conceived. Its birth was still nearly nine months away — at the feast of Pentecost — but this extraordinary moment is also the beginning of Jesus' frontal challenge to the powers of hell.

50.
Genesis 6:2

51.
Genesis 6:4

The Near Future

The Jewish name for *hell* or *Hades* was 'Sheol'. The Greek conception of the underworld was much like a multi-layered dungeon — far below the realm of Hades lay Tartarus where, according to the apostle Peter, the Watcher angels who plotted together at Mount Hermon were imprisoned.[53]

Sheol is a complex word, deriving from the Hebrew for *desire* or *ask*. A close relative of it is the personal name, Saul, which also comes from this root.

Just a few years after Jesus made this momentous announcement at Caesarea Philippi, a zealous young firebrand would have passed by here on his way to Damascus. Archaeological diggings have shown that shrine of Pan was right next to the main road inland from the coast. Saul, in possession of warrants for the arrests of the Christians of Damascus, would have trod this road en route to his encounter with the resurrected Jesus. The same Jesus who had said that the gates (*judges... judgments*) of Hades (*Sheol...Saul*) would not prevail against His church.

No wonder Saul was stricken blind not far from here. The land was so deeply healed by Jesus that the judgments of Saul — the bindings and loosings of the legal injunctions he held — were simply not tenable. They fell down in the spirit, just as he fell down in the physical.

52.
Ernst Wilhelm Hengstenberg, *Dissertations on the Genuineness of the Pentateuch*, Volume 2 (1847).

53.
2 Peter 2:4 and 1 Enoch 20:2. (Kelley Coblentz Bautch, *A Study of the Geography of 1 Enoch 17–19: 'No One Has Seen what I Have Seen'*, Brill 2003

CELEBRATING THE DAY

Mount Hermon is one of the few places in Israel which remains snow-covered all year round. The lower slopes are subject to 'kaphowr', *frost*.

Perhaps because of its action of *covering* the landscape with a veil of white purity, *frost* is derived from the word for *atonement*, 'kaphar'. There is a wide range of meanings and senses in 'kaphar': *cover, coat, coat with pitch, make atonement, to reconcile, purge, pacify, propitiate, forgive, be merciful, cleanse, appease, pardon* and *put off*.

It is not only the root of *frost*, but also:

- 'kapporeth' — the *mercy-seat* on the Ark of the Covenant and the place of atoning sacrifice within the Holy of Holies

- 'kippur' — as in Yom Kippur, the Day of *Atonement*, the only day the high priest could enter the Holy of Holies

- 'kopher' — *ransom, redemption price, price of a life, bribe*

- 'kaphar' — *a village, a place to seek shelter or cover*

- 'kephir' — *a young lion*

- 'kippah' — *a cap without a brim to cover the crown of the head,*[54] *a skullcap*

- 'kaphowr' — *a basin* (especially a shallow basin carved into the 'kaph', *cornerstone* or *threshold stone* at the entrance to a house)[55]

- 'Kaypha' or 'Cephas' — the name given to Simon by Jesus, meaning *cornerstone*[56] or *threshold stone*

- 'Caiaphas' — the name of the high priest in the time of Jesus

---

54.
The English word *cap* may come from 'kippah'. See Isaac Mozeson, *The Word: The Dictionary that Reveals the Hebrew Source of English*, SPI Books 2001

55.
The English word *cup* may come from 'kaph'. (Ibid.)

56.
Famously, Psalm 118:22 NAS says: *'The stone which the builders rejected has become the chief cornerstone,'* and by establishing the cornerstone for His church as He identifies Himself with the scapegoat, Jesus nuances His words with a subtle prophecy: the church can expect rejection from the world.

Yom Kippur was the only day of the year that the high priest entered the veil into the Holy of Holies as the mediator between God and the people. He would offer incense, representing the prayers of the priests, sacrifice a bull for his own sins as well as those of his household. In addition, lots would be used to select a goat to be sacrificed and another to receive the sins of the people. The blood of the sacrificed goat would be sprinkled seven times on the mercy-seat. The other goat would be led away — to die. During the era of Moses, in the time of the desert wanderings, this second goat — the scapegoat — would instead be led out a three days' journey into the wilderness. There it would be abandoned — never to return.

By specifically heading out to a place notorious for goat-demons along with a shrine to a goat deity, Jesus evoked the imagery of the scapegoat. Two years prior, on the day after a previous Yom Kippur, John the Baptist had identified Jesus as the Lamb of God. Jesus was now expanding the understanding of His disciples and letting them know He was also the scapegoat — destined to die. Simon was so reluctant to accept this that Jesus rebuked him in no uncertain terms.

This reprimand took place just moments after Jesus undertook a name covenant[57] with him. They exchanged names: Simon, an unschooled fisherman of Galilee, gave Jesus the title 'Messiah' and

'It will carry all the people's sins...
into a desolate land...'
Leviticus 16:22 NLT

Jesus gave him in return 'Cephas', a Hebrew name whose closest Greek equivalent is Petros, *rock*.[58] Cephas was essentially the same name as that of the high priest at the time, and it allows us a glimpse into the divine destiny given to Caiaphas — if only he'd chosen to follow his true calling. He should have been the first to proclaim the Messiah.

Back in the time before the exodus from Egypt, the firstborn of families had the right to be priests in their own household. However as a result of the rebellion against God involving the sin of the golden calf, this privilege was lost. Instead when the Levites sided with Moses and punished the people's defiance of God, they were granted the right to be priests for the entire nation. The privilege of being high priest was further restricted, within the Levite tribe, to the line of Aaron.

However, when the kingdom of David divided into Judah and Israel, two camps of rival high priests came about: in Jerusalem, those from the line of Aaron, and in Dan, those descended from Moses.[59]

So when Jesus gave Simon the fisherman the name of the high priest, He was prophesying that the right to be priests in your own household was about to return. Did He mean this right to be restricted to Simon Peter and perhaps the rest of the disciples? I think Peter's own words on what the cornerstone and the priesthood mean should be the ultimate testimony here. They are recorded in 1 Peter 2:4–10 and there he makes it clear what He understood Jesus was saying.

When Jesus restored the priesthood, it wasn't as a gift to the line of Aaron or the line of Moses. Or even back, as it was originally, to fathers and husbands. It was a gift to all believers.

'...the desert will rejoice and blossom'
Isaiah 35:1 BSB

57.
Anne Hamilton, *Name Covenant: Invitation to Friendship — Strategies for the Threshold #3*, Armour Books 2018

58.
More accurately, it's *the rock from which an enterprise is started*. The English variant of this is, of course, Peter. However, 'peter' is a Hebrew word in its own right, meaning *firstborn* or *the one who opens the way*.

59.
Judges 18:30

& Prayer:

Father God — Daddy God — You blessed Your sons to be the spiritual leaders in our homes. We ask Your forgiveness for our disobedience and for taking that privilege for granted.

We thank You that Jesus did not abandon us and leave us without a priest to mediate on our behalf. We thank You that He is the Good Shepherd who does not leave us wandering in our own lostness. We praise You that He healed and restored and blessed us beyond our wildest dreams.

Daddy God, so often we've failed to acknowledge or even notice what Jesus has done. Forgive us for our blindness. Forgive us for our ingratitude. Heal and restore our sight and give us a resilient attitude of gratitude so that we appreciate and recognise Your healing, restoring power and saving action in our lives. Give us an appreciation of what an awesome life-transforming responsibility it is to have spiritual headship in our homes, our workplaces and our churches. Transform us so that, Your grace shining through us, we can be Your co-labourers in transforming the homes of this nation. Let it be accomplished by the power of Your Word. May we become what we already are — sons and daughters of the most high God — ready, willing and able to do Your will.

Daddy God — *Abba* — Jesus healed and restored history, giving back to me a spiritual headship in my particular sphere of responsibility. Thank You for the honour You give me in entrusting me with this task. I ask Your help in ensuring the light and life of Jesus shines through me, so that everyone I encounter has the opportunity to answer Jesus' question for themselves: 'Who do YOU say I am?'

Help me, Lord, to stop evading and avoiding and side-stepping that question so that I can help others too. Help me say with conviction: 'Jesus, You are the Messiah, sent from God. Yes, You are the very Son of God.'

I do believe, Lord. But there are parts of my heart that don't fully trust You. Help my unbelief. Jesus, as the High Priest forever, heal my heart and heal my family so I can advance Your kingdom and fulfil my role in your royal priesthood.

I ask this in Your name. Amen.

The Meaning of 'Hermon'

The many possibilities for this name include *anathema* with the dual meaning of *forever accursed* as well as *dedicated to God* — as in *devoted to total destruction*.

Its variety of names testify to its importance for different peoples and in different cultures. It has at least twenty ancient temples on its slopes. The Sidonians called it 'Sirion' (Psalm 29:6) meaning *breastplate* or *little prince* and the Amorites called it 'Senir', *snow mountain* or *be pointed, spiky* deriving from 'tsinnah', meaning *piercing, hook, barb, coldness* (of snow), *shield* or *buckler*. (Deuteronomy 3:8–9)

Hermon is also said to derive from 'kermone', *abrupt* or *peak of a mountain* (eteacherhebrew.com) or possibly mean *sacred* (New Advent Catholic Encyclopedia and biblehub.com) or *sanctuary* (thebiblejourney.org). Other suggestions include: *net* from 'haram' or *sickle* from 'hermesh' (Hebrew and Aramaic Dictionary of the Old Testament, Fohrer et al.).

The oldest Hebrew name for it was Sion, *lifted up* from 'nasa", *lift, banner*. It was called Mount Lebanon by Josephus, a name meaning *brick* or *white* (by implication *transparent, paved*), from 'laben', t*o be white, transparent, pure* (related to 'lebonah', *frankincense*).

Amongst its Arabic names are Jabel A-talg, *snow mountain* and Jebel esh-Sheik, *chief mountain*. In Chaldean, it was also called *snowy mountain:* Tûr Telga.

Jim Stinehart (ibiblio.org) comments that the most likely general meaning is *the high place* but more accurately, from the true root, M-N, it would be *appointed to oversee,* having implications of *towering, divine-like grandeur*.

Since the since the Yom Kippur War in 1973, Israel has considered Mount Hermon with its detection array as the 'eyes of the State'. Hermon in English is a homonym for 'herman', *army protection*.

'...if you have faith the size of a mustard seed, you can say to this mountain, "Move from here to there," and it will move.'

Matthew 17:22 BSB

Discussion Questions:

(1) Which particular healing aspect of the history of Caesarea Philippi speaks most strongly to you?

(2) The layers and levels of healing in just a few words from Jesus are so complex we've probably only scratched the surface we know about. Even so, we can see some of what Jesus spoke about. As you look at His words and reflect on what they are designed to achieve, how would they influence your own prayer life?

(3) Do you think name covenants still occur today?

(4) Do you suffer from panic attacks? How do the words of Jesus address this issue?

(5) Many families have a designated 'scapegoat'. When we take on this role, it's because we do not truly believe in Jesus as the scapegoat and the all-sufficiency of His atoning sacrifice. When we project this role onto others, it's also because we do not truly believe in Jesus as the scapegoat and the all-sufficiency of His atoning sacrifice. How should family behaviour change in the light of what Jesus has accomplished for us?

Rose of Sharon:

from Hebrew, *overshadowed by God's love*

from Hebrew, *the name of a plain,* **but poetically nuanced with** *righteousness, justice, breastplate, armour, gate, judgment, song.*

The sons of God saw that
the daughters of men were beautiful and desirable;
and they took wives for themselves, whomever they chose.

Genesis 6:2 AMP

Mark 9:2 NRS

Six days later,
Jesus took with Him Peter and James and John,
and led them up on a high mountain apart,
by themselves. And He was transfigured before them.

Weight of Glory

This narrative account of the events surrounding the transfiguration of Jesus is told from the perspective of the apostle John. It takes the view this event was a fulfilment of the prophecy of Psalm 82 and, as a logical consequence, it therefore has to have occurred on Mount Hermon.

I'm not quite sure why some people think I should have included my own eye-witness account of the mountaintop experience. Perhaps it's curiosity — or perhaps it's the vague feeling that the retellings of Matthew, Mark and Luke somehow lack the authenticity of a first-hand report.

Actually the fact that all three of them are a step or two removed from the action is a distinct advantage: they don't look at their own words and despair of how pitiful and inadequate they are. I marvel at how they've managed to communicate some of the wonder of an event that still leaves me struggling for a remotely fitting description. Even after all this time, I am still tongue-tangled and inarticulate with the sheer indescribable weight of glory revealed to us.

And even though I applaud Peter's depiction as superb, it still doesn't convey the spine-tingling splendour of that moment when the cloud came down, radiant with beauty and effulgent with light. I guess you had to be there. Sure, I admit he comes very close with this: *'For when He received honour and glory from God the Father, and the voice was borne to Him by the Majestic Glory,* "This is My beloved Son, with whom I am well pleased," *we ourselves heard this very voice borne from heaven, for we were with Him on the holy mountain.'*[1]

By 'we', Peter means himself and my brother James and me. We fulfilled the ancient requirement for two or three witnesses. So, let me confirm what he's written as accurate. And what Matthew, Mark and Luke have added too.

1.
2 Peter 1:17–18 ESV

A psalm of Asaph

God stands in the divine assembly;
He administers judgment in the midst of the gods.
'How long will you judge unjustly
and show favouritism to the wicked?' Selah
'Judge on behalf of the helpless and the orphan;
provide justice to the afflicted and the poor.
Rescue the helpless and the needy;
deliver them from the hand of the wicked.'

Psalm 82:1–8 LEB

They do not know or consider.
They go about in the darkness,
so that all the foundations of the earth are shaken.
I have said, 'You are gods,
and sons of the Most High, all of you.
However, you will die like men,
and you will fall like one of the princes.'
Rise up, O God, judge the earth,
because You shall inherit all the nations.

And although I don't want to alter anything, I'd nevertheless like to explain some things. I hope to clarify some aspects and nuances that seem to have been lost in translation. First of all, I'd like to say one thing about Jesus. It's this: in human terms, He's Jewish. That might seem obvious but it's all too easy to overlook the implications of this fact. He was part of the culture He was born into and so He spoke, not only in parables, but also in *remez*: subtle hints, refined allusions, delicate clues, indirect references. These *remez* no doubt seem inscrutable, if you're used to brash, blunt speech.

So let me unlock some of the mysteries of the *remez* that we walked into that day we climbed the mountain with Him.

Now it generally escapes people's attention that Jesus had actually declared war on the Day of Atonement, Yom Kippur. He had officially put the angels of the nations on notice when, together with the rest of the disciples, we'd gathered at Caesarea Philippi.[2] There, at the foot of the mountain, in front of the temple to the goat-demon Pan of the Greeks, Jesus made an incredibly provocative announcement: His bride — His church, His ekklesia, His called-out ones — were

2.
Back in the time of Moses and Joshua, this was the site of a temple to Baal-Gad: a godling whose name meant *master of fortune* or *of troops*. Its double meaning may have come about through the thought that fortune in war often depended, humanly speaking, on the quality of the troops that could be mustered. Something of a pun on the Hebrew word, 'gedi', *young goat*, might have made it a natural choice for a sacrificial shrine to the half-human half-goat Pan.

destined to replace the unholy and unrighteous representatives in God's existing heavenly assembly. She would be handed the keys of government and given the legislative power to bind and loose in accordance with the will of the Most High. The unjust judges of the Divine Council were therefore formally warned that their time was just about up.

I must admit that, until I was actually on my way up the mountain with Peter and James, I hadn't realised that we were the advance force of Jesus' full frontal assault on the angels of the nations in the Great Assembly. I simply didn't put two and two together.

When Jesus had alluded to law-making — binding and loosing — we were still thinking earthly political legislature. We still had it locked in our heads that He was about to kick the Romans out of the country. All it needed was for Him to declare Himself and there would be thousands join His uprising. We weren't sure if He was the war messiah or the kingly messiah but, to us, it didn't really matter.

So it didn't occur to any of us Jesus was speaking spiritually about government. Nor did it dawn on us that He was actually taking us up into the heart of hell's counterfeit council chambers to get His decree ratified. Luke makes the point of mentioning that Peter was completely clueless but the fact is we all were. Sure, we realised the

'After six days Jesus ... led them up a high mountain...'
Matthew 17:1 BSB

significance of the mountain: that was inescapable. About the time we reached the snowline, it dawned on us that we were going to the top. It also dawned on us that this was the peak where the 'young lions', the seventy sons of the pagan goddess Asherah, had their palatial residences. Yes, Jesus was taking us to beard the young lions in their own den!

In other circumstances, I might have been worried. But Jesus had already shown up Asherah as a second-rate counterfeit when He'd walked on water. He'd also made it clear that Asherah's consort Tammuz wasn't entitled to the name 'Bread Come Down From Heaven' when He'd multiplied the loaves and fishes.

'...they remembered their altars and their Asherah poles beside green trees on the high hills.'

Jeremiah 17:2 ISV

'...He will command His angels ... to guard you in all your ways.'

Psalm 91:11 NIV

Now He'd prepared us to move against the seventy young lions. And He spoke His own government into being to counter this false regime. You see, seventy has long been the full number of appointees for divine government — for God's assembly. It's been that way even before Moses took the seventy elders up onto God's sapphire floor for a state banquet. In fact Moses himself testified that the tradition was ancient even in his time[3] — that it was set according to the angelic principalities who ruled the nations.

We were in the right territory. Enoch, the seventh descendent in the line of Adam, wrote in his scroll that he'd been sitting by the waters of Dan when he heard the weeping of the seventy shepherd-angels of the nations. And he had prophesied that they would be punished along with the Watchers who fathered the giants.[4]

And those Watchers had descended onto the very mountain we were ascending.[5]

James and I had sensed the governmental aspect of Jesus' words and actions. What we failed to understand was the kind of administration He expected of us. We began nursing daydreams of ourselves, one at His right hand, one at His left. We would be dispensers of justice and truth, mercy and peace. There would be no bribes or currying of favour with us. We'd lift some up, we'd put some down. But it would all be impartial and honourable.

3.
Comment on Deuteronomy 32:7–9 in Walter Wink, *Naming the Powers: The Language of Power in the New Testament, Volume 1,* Fortress Press 1984

4.
Walter Wink, *Naming the Powers: The Language of Power in the New Testament, Volume 1,* Fortress Press 1984

5.
North. The word is 'zaphon'. The Canaanites of old had maintained the seventy brothers of Baal had their residences within a palatial abode on Mount Zaphon. They located Zaphon far up along the coast, but many commentators note how fluid geography is when it comes to sacred mountains. Even Mount Zion gets 'zaphon' attached to it. (Psalm 48:2) However I think Jesus knew that its true location was Mount Hermon.

'I see the branch of an almond tree'
... The Lord said to me,
'You have seen correctly,
for I am watching
to see that My word
is fulfilled.'
Jeremiah 1:11–12 NIV

Our lesson was swift in coming. Just a few days later our illusions were brutally cut short. After coming down the mountain we went to go through Samaritan territory but, unlike our previous welcome, we were made to feel unwanted. James and I were so offended by their attitude we wanted to call down fire from heaven. Oh yes, we knew we could do it. After all Elijah had — and we'd just been treated as equals in his company back on the mountain.

But, as soon as we suggested it, Jesus told us off. And in no uncertain terms!

It was the public humiliation we needed. Not just James and me but all of us. All seventy of us. Even as we were still smarting from the rebuke, we were restored. Jesus is forever like that. He gathered the seventy of us — yes, seventy, just so the most dim-witted of us could understand He was creating the earthly counterpart of His Father's Divine Council — and then sent us out to the villages round about. You've got to smile: the word for *villages* in old Hebrew is the same as that for *young lions*.

We were being sent out as sheep amongst wolves. Or more accurately perhaps, amongst *young lions*. The principalities had their eyes on us. Our mission: to heal the sick and to announce, 'The kingdom of God has come near you.' Yes, this was the practical outworking of the first law of His new government: Love God with your whole being. And the second law: love others, treating them as you yourself would like to be treated.

When we came back, telling Him how wonderfully well it had all gone, He told us He'd seen the satan — the lord of all the principalities — hurtling down from heaven to inspect the damage we were doing. And then He authorised us to take even further steps against the greater powers — not simply against the young lions, but against the higher levels of darkness symbolised by serpents and scorpions: Python, the spirit of constriction and divination, as well as Leviathan, the spirit of retaliation.

Yet, He warned us not to rejoice such angelic commanders submitted to us, but that our names were written in heaven.

Yes, our names were written in the scrolls of heaven. This brings me to another aspect of the *remez*. The incident on the mountain was not just about government, it was about names and the identity that lies in the heart of the cornerstone.

When the Spirit of God hovers over our unformed state, whispering our name at the moment of conception in our mother's womb, He breathes a soul into us. Woven into that name is identity and destiny.

In fact, the giving of a name is the impartation of a calling. But impartation is only part of the story. Without implantation, all is lost. Think of it this way: im*part*ation is necessary for conception, im*plant*ation is necessary for a viable pregnancy.

That's why we were on the mountain: Jesus had imparted the name and now He wanted it to be implanted. He had breathed a soul into His church with the name He had given: we were to be the living stones built on the Cornerstone.

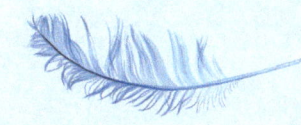

'Who do you say that I am?' Jesus had asked all of us when we'd been at the foot of the mountain in front of Pan's aptly named Gates of Hell.

Simon had answered that He was the Messiah and the name covenant occurred with its exchange of identities. Simon had received a new name. In Greek it was Petros, *the rock*. But not just any rock: one from which an enterprise is started. It was a pun on our Hebrew word, 'peter', *the one who opens the way*. However, the Aramaic

name Jesus gave him was Cephas, *the cornerstone*. The same name as that of the high priest Caiaphas.

This was the background to our ascent of the mountain. It turned out Jesus had taken us there to be witnesses to His Father's answer to His question: 'Who do you say that I am?'

Yes, His Father's answer! 'This is My Son, My Chosen One; listen to Him!'⁶

Remez upon *remez* upon *remez* was hidden in those few words. 'This is My Son' alludes to the words of the second psalm: 'You are My Son… ask Me and I will make the nations Your inheritance.'⁷ God was not only announcing that the scapegoat, the rejected one, the unwanted Cornerstone was His beloved, He was counter-signing the declaration of war Jesus had made. We were there to begin the government that would inherit the nations.

And just to make it really sure we got it, God directed our attention to the prophecy of Isaiah: 'Here is My Servant, whom I uphold, My Chosen One, in whom My soul delights. I will put My Spirit on Him, and He will bring justice to the nations.'⁸ Look at that reference to the Chosen One. Notice what the delight is all about: the coming of justice to the nations. Again it's about despoiling the seventy young lions — the angel-shepherds of the nations, the principalities of this world, the enemy government with its dark councils and schemes of destruction.

And finally God confirms what Simon Peter said: that Jesus is the Messiah. 'Listen to Him!' comes from the words of Moses, the first messiah of Israel. *'The Lord your God will raise up for you a prophet like me from among your own brothers. You must listen to him.'*⁹

There it was: the command to listen to Him. In our day, 'a prophet like Moses' simply meant the Messiah — the one who would bring us out of the slavery imposed on us by a foreign nation. Not Egypt this time, but Rome. God had declared to us that the prophecy of Moses was fulfilled in the flesh in front of us. And again, in context, the words of Scripture were about the dispossession of the nations: *'The nations you will dispossess listen to those who practice sorcery or*

6.
Luke 9:31 ESV

7.
Psalm 2:7–8 NIV

8.
Isaiah 42:1 BSB

9.
Deuteronomy 15:18 HCSB

divination. But as for you, the Lord your God has not permitted you to do so. The Lord your God will raise up for you a prophet like me from among you, from your fellow Israelites. You must listen to Him.'[10]

Moses was with us on the mountain. Elijah was there too. A witness to the words of the last book of the Torah quoted by God, as well as a witness to the writings of the prophets quoted by God.

Jesus went to the mountain in order to fulfil the prophecy of Asaph's psalm: *'God stands in the divine assembly; He administers judgment in the midst of the gods.'*[11] He stood in the Council, was introduced by the Father Himself, was accompanied into the assembly chambers by two of the greatest figures in our history, was declared the Father's beloved and Chosen One, was proclaimed as the One to listen to, was promised that His church would be brought forth at the appointed time.

Just under nine months away.

God alluded to that when He quoted from Psalm 2: 'You are My son.' The very next words are: 'Today I have become Your Father.'[12] But there is a deeper meaning here. Hebrew is a heavily nuanced

10.
Deuteronomy 15:17–18 NIV
The angels of the nations were renowned for teaching sorcery.

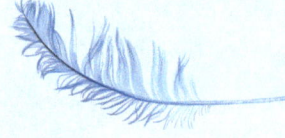

11.
Psalm 82:1 LEB

'...tear out the fangs of the young lions, o Lord...'
Psalm 58:6 ESV

language, and this phrase also means: 'Today I am presenting you.'[12] These are the words of a midwife, taking delivery of a child and holding Him up for everyone to see.

On the mountain, God presented His Son to the angels of the nations, to the cloud of witnesses who had gone before and to those of us who represented Israel. He was showing Him off to the entire cosmos.

And in using the words of a midwife, He prophesied a birth for those who did what He asked: those who listened to Him.

Peter might have had a brain fumble when he started talking about setting up tents and tabernacles. But he was no less clueless — but nevertheless prophetic — than his namesake Caiaphas.

It was the feast of tabernacles — Sukkot — the day this all happened, a time when we commemorate the years of God's provision in the wilderness by building and living in simple booth-like shelters. It's a season of joy; a foretaste of the age of the Messiah when there will be peace on earth and all nations will live together in harmony under the canopy of His glory.

Make no mistake, beloved ones of Jesus, He healed history that day when He climbed Mount Hermon. He stitched up a great rent which had torn apart the entire world from the time the watcher-angels had descended there, on that very peak, in the time of Jared.

But His healing was both once and future: the time will come again when the angels of the nations will gather their locust-swarm forces here, to swing down from the north to attack His bride. But, as He promised, these dark principalities will not prevail.

They may pluck up a stitch or two in their efforts to rip up His seamless repair—and that He then calls us to work with Him to mend. We are called to 'tikkun olam', not simply *mending the world* but *mending the age*.

12. Psalm 2:7 GNT

Notes

The story of the Transfiguration is told in three of the four gospels.

    Matthew 17:1–11

    Mark 9:2–12

    Luke 9:28–36

It may seem surprising that John, the only actual eyewitness amongst the gospel writers, didn't record his own perspective on it. Perhaps that's why I chose to put the narrative above in his viewpoint.

As it happens, slightly different wording is given in each of the re-tellings of Matthew, Mark and Luke. They in turn are marginally different from the words recorded by Peter in his epistle.

    2 Peter 1:16–21

These slight differences are perfectly natural in my view — and, to me, evidence of the truthfulness of the accounts, not a reason to suspect them. Each writer is translating Hebrew words into Greek — and so, because languages don't have a one-to-one correspondence and also because writers are unlikely to think in exactly the same way when it comes to translating highly nuanced words, small differences should be expected as a matter of course. However, these differences should be insignificant when it comes to the idea being conveyed. They should enhance one another, not detract from one another.

This is exactly what happens. Many scholars believe the unnamed mountain in all of these writings is Tabor. I don't think this is possible, despite the weight of tradition attached to it. Because of all of the long and deep history of Mount Hermon that I've presented in the narrative above, as well as its proximity to Caesarea Philippi — which is specifically identified by both Matthew and Mark as being the whereabouts of Jesus six days prior to the Transfiguration — I believe it has to be the site of this revelation.

'...we ourselves heard this voice from heaven when we were with Him on the holy mountain.'

2 Peter 1:18 BSB

I would like to put on record my deep indebtedness to Dwight Pryor and the profound insights he uncovered in writing of the *remez* encoded in God's declaration about Jesus.[13] I have followed his lead quite closely in opening out the subtle references to the Scriptures from Psalm 2, Isaiah 41 and Deuteronomy 15. As he points out, God quotes from each of the three significant sections of the Hebrew Scriptures: His selections come from the Torah (the five books of Moses), the Nevi'im (the prophets) and the Ketuvim (the holy writings). I am also indebted to Pryor for mentioning Dr Lindsay's alternative reading of the words, 'This day I have begotten you,' as the declaration of a midwife: 'This day I am presenting you.'

In the context of the conception of the church on Yom Kippur and its birth on the Feast of Pentecost nearly nine months later, this 'midwifery' event on Mount Hermon corresponds to 'implantation'. There is a parallel in human gestation — a fertilised egg needs to be implanted in the womb about six days after conception. The significance of 'six days' in terms of the time differential between a name covenant and a threshold covenant is detailed in *God's Pottery*.[14] It harks back to the events of the creation week outlined in Genesis. However, in the particular instance under consideration here, the name covenant occurs at Caesarea Philippi when Jesus and Simon exchange names while the threshold covenant occurs on the mountaintop.

Jesus had more than one agenda when He climbed Mount Hermon: He was intent on fulfilling the prophecy of Psalm 82 and to do that He had to stand in the 'council of the gods'. It was therefore necessary to go to their designated place of assembly. A second item on His agenda was ensuring the birth of His church was on track. He had first imparted existence to the church through His words of conception six days previously. So this was the appropriate time interval for implantation. Thirdly, He was setting His government into place at the very same location as the angelic principalities had refined their plans for global domination. He was supplanting them with a kingdom of love and justice. Fourthly, He was seeking confirmation of the identity of the church He was founding. Its calling came from its covenant with Him and His covenant with the Father.

Craig Hill of *Family Foundations* says that when a Hebrew boy reached the same age and was ready for his bar mitzvah — the ceremony where he would become *a son of the covenant*[15] — the boy's father would lift him high on his shoulders and run around the village in celebration, shouting to the cheers of uncles and cousins: 'This is my beloved son, in whom I am well-pleased.'

13.
Dwight Pryor, *Jesus—The Fullness of Tanakh*, in John Fieldsend, Clifford Hill, Walter Riggans, John CP Smith, Fred Wright (editors), *Roots and Branches: Explorations into the Jewish Context of the Christian Faith*, PWM Trust 1998

'God takes His stand in the divine assembly; among the divine beings He renders judgment.'

Psalm 82:1 ISV

These words are precisely reflected in Peter's translation of God's declaration on the mountain. Jesus was declared a son of the covenant, even as He was raising a covenant on behalf of His church. His kinsmen were with Him: Moses, Elijah, James, John and Peter. They may not have been cheering, but consider the messages Jesus had given them over the previous week. Back down the mountain at Caesarea Philippi, He had used a range of symbolism to declare Himself the scapegoat of Yom Kippur. He'd also given Simon the name 'Cephas', *cornerstone*, effectively claiming as His own name along with the right to bestow it where He chose. Yet the Cornerstone was well-known as the stone that had been rejected.

14.
Anne Hamilton, *God's Pottery: The Sea of Names and the Pierced Inheritance*, Armour Books 2016

15.
'Bar mitzvah' means *son of the covenant*.

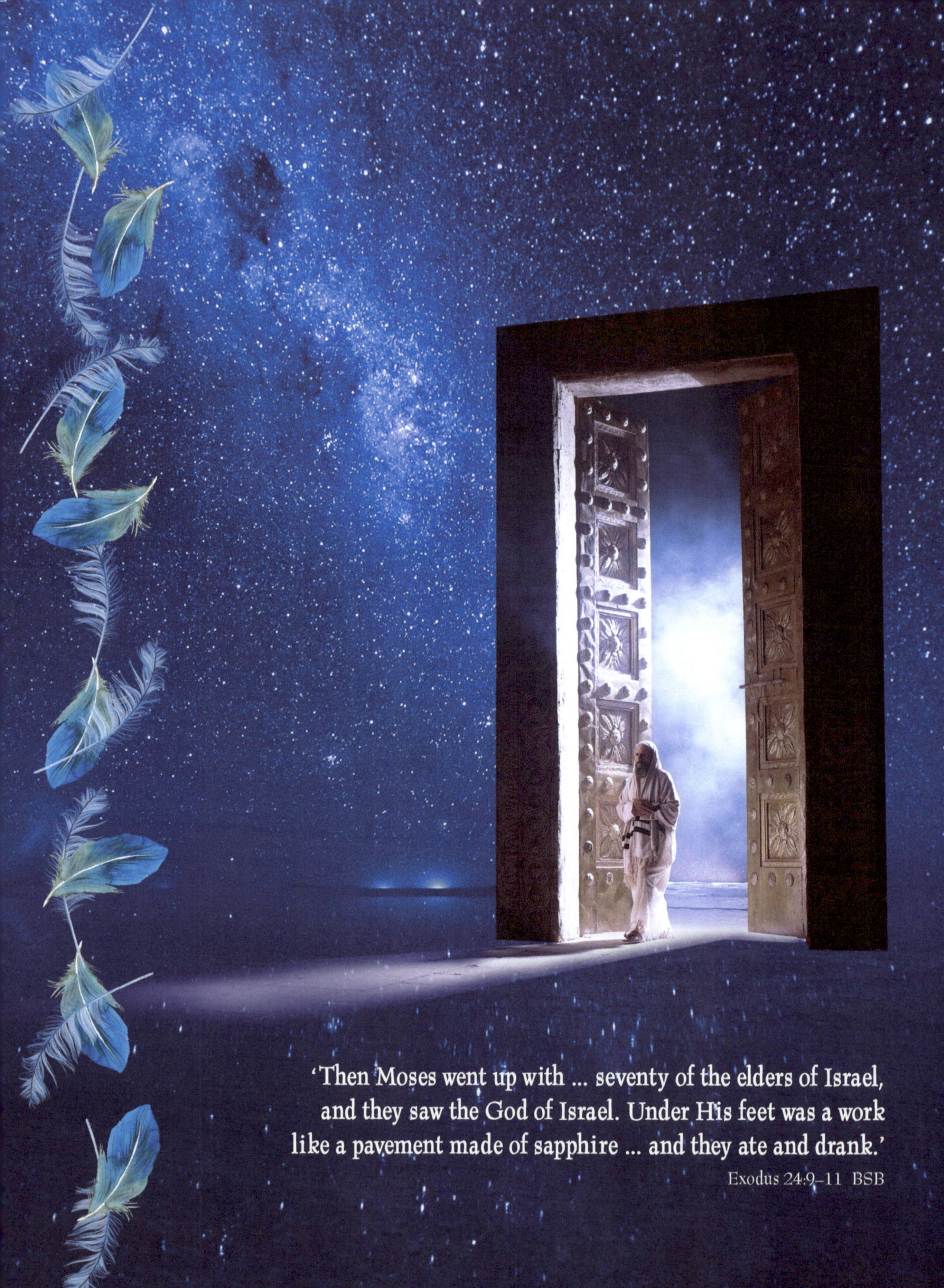

So the message He had delivered at the Gates of Hell was rejection, rejection and more rejection.

He could have done what we do when we're rejected. He could have fled from it. Or He could have shrugged His shoulders and ignored it. But He did neither. He accepted the rejection, walked into the heart of it, and found His identity as the beloved of the Father.

If there is a lesson here for us today, it's this: whether we use various coping mechanisms to handle rejection or whether we run from it, neither is any use. It's only when we unite ourselves in the covenantal oneness with the Rejected One and climb the mountain with Him that we will find ourselves wrapped in His cloud-canopy and find ourselves accepted as the Beloved.

Prayer:

Father God:

> Your Son — Your beloved Son with whom You are well pleased — was a son of Jewish soil. Just as we are part of the land where we live and just as we are steeped in the culture of our time, so was He. Father, forgive us for our disregard for who Jesus is and for His culture and race. Give us an awareness of the enormity of our sin of dishonour and disrespect for Jews and Jewish culture which has extended over so many millennia. We have sinned, Father, both as individuals and collectively as the church Your Son built on the Rock the builders had rejected. Awaken our spirit, Lord, and grant to us the gift of repentance and the ability to make a 180 degree turn. Grant that we may hear You say: 'Today, you have become My child in a new way. I am well pleased with you.'
>
> Protect us, Father, from any retaliation and backlash by the 'young lions' of the spirit realm which might be the result of our sin. Kiss us, Father, and clothe us in Your armour.

Daddy God:

> To call You 'Daddy' means we have divested ourselves of all ideas of greatness. It is to know we have no power except that which comes from You. It means we acknowledge we are at best children in Your kindergarten — in a sort of pre-school and preparation for all the wonders and greatness that lie ahead. We are, in fact, a people blessed beyond measure. Teach us, Daddy, to appreciate the blessing of Your Son and our Brother, Jesus, who willingly divested Himself of all that He was, so that we can become the very best that we are.
>
> What a Saviour we have! Thank You, Jesus. Thank You. Thank You.

Father God:

> Jesus asked You to forgive us because we do not know what we do. He is so right. We are ignorant of what we do and why we do it. We reject. We are rejected. Rejection seems to be the theme and the bane of this century. All the self-focus, narcissism and foibles of the 'me' generation have spread to all. Ads want me to believe I deserve the best: 'Because I am worth it.'
>
> Keep me mindful I am only 'worth it' because of who Jesus is and what He did for me.
>
> We have come to believe that because we 'feel' something it really is true for no reason other than we 'feel' it. Sometimes feelings are liars. How many times do we 'feel' rejected and so react sinfully to an innocent situation. We have pre-set tapes always on the ready to respond to any rejection emergency.
>
> Father, carry me out of the satan's camp! I confess my self-focus and obsession with rejection. Jesus was rejected but He did not react — He acted. Father, right now I make a conscious decision to come out of agreement with the satan; I accept Your forgiveness and I ask Your help to walk in Your gift of freedom and total acceptance.

Daddy God:

> It is Your will I come into the fullness of my birthright. I know this cannot happen until I am healed in body, mind and spirit. This healing cannot happen until I become Your very best for me — the person You meant me to be when You whispered into my soul at conception. I need healing of body, mind and spirit before I can be Your very best. Lord, I want to be that person — help my inability. I believe, Father — help my unbelief.

I have had glimpses, Lord, but the fullness of who I am escapes me. I have experienced enough to know there will be an explosion of life as the floodgates of heaven open. My life will never again be the same. I will do and be what You predestined for me to do and be. This is Your desire, not just for me, but for the whole human race. Father, I accept Your healing — help my inability to fully accept it; help me through my unbelief to belief. May Your Kingdom come on earth as it is in heaven.

In the name of Jesus of Nazareth, the Rejected One.

Amen

'...under His wings you will find refuge...'
Psalm 91:4 BSB

Discussion Questions:

(1) How do you deal with rejection? Do you just handle it? Do you flee from it? Do you reject others before they can reject you? In the light of the example of Jesus, what changes can you make to your behaviour?

(2) Moses died on a mountain outside Israel, on the east bank of the Jordan. He saw the Promised Land from afar but was not allowed to enter it. All because he struck a rock. But this was not a trivial action: it was a well-known symbol of refusing covenant — therefore he was one of the builders who rejected the Cornerstone. What does it tell you about God that Moses was invited as a witness to this meeting on this mountain inside Israel?

(3) Who do you say that Jesus is?

Coda

When Moses descended the mountain, out of the cloud of glory, he discovered that the hearts of the people of Israel festered with faithlessness and perversion. They'd built the golden calf, participating in idolatrous worship.

When Jesus descended the mountain, out of the cloud of glory, He discovered that things hadn't changed — even with the passage of millennia. The hearts of the people of Israel still festered with faithlessness and perversion.

Let's pick up the story in Luke 9:37, just following the transfiguration:

'The next day, when they came down from the mountain, a large crowd met Him. A man in the crowd called out, "Teacher, I beg you to look at my son, for he is my only child. A spirit seizes him and he suddenly screams; it throws him into convulsions so that he foams at the mouth. It scarcely ever leaves him and is destroying him. I begged your disciples to drive it out, but they could not."

"You unbelieving and perverse generation," Jesus replied, "how long shall I stay with you and put up with you? Bring your son here."

Even while the boy was coming, the demon threw him to the ground in a convulsion. But Jesus rebuked the impure spirit, healed the boy and gave him back to his father. And they were all amazed at the greatness of God.'

Later on, the disciples ask Jesus why they were so ineffective. He tells them that the kind of spirit they were dealing with only comes out by prayer and fasting. Now, many people are under the impression that Jesus was speaking about His disciples when He said, '*You unbelieving and perverse generation*,' but I don't think that's the case at all. He was speaking to the father.

The accusation is harsh, but not without warrant. Jesus had just come down the mountain and rejoined the disciples He'd left behind. He had therefore returned to Caesarea Philippi. He was back at the Gates of Hell.

So what on earth was a Jewish father doing at a pagan shrine with a boy who, in modern understanding, would be suffering from epilepsy? The answer is simple enough. In ancient times, epilepsy was called 'panolepsy' and was understood to mean the afflicted person was possessed by Pan. The father was therefore at Caesarea Philippi for no other purpose than to make sacrificial offerings in order to secure a cure for his son. He was about to engage — indeed, perhaps had already engaged — in idolatrous worship.

Pan has many other names. In some cultures, he is benign, in others malignant. But, whatever he is known as, his agenda is the same — to cause us to panic; to flee from rejection into a false refuge; to tempt us to wish instead of pray; to lure us into word-binding rather than allowing Jesus to rebuke him; to hunt after us in order to undo the good that we do for the Kingdom.

This is the threshold guardian who wants to undo the healing of history that we bring to birth on behalf of the Lord.

It is not up to us to seal the healing. That is the work of the Holy Spirit. But it may be up to us to ask Him to brood upon the waters of conception and overshadow them with His love.

Accepting Jesus as the Messiah

Father in heaven, I mourn for my separation from You. I have grieved You in doing what has caused You pain, my family and friends unbearable loss, and the world harm. The damage to my own soul is incalculable.

The wounds that should have been mine in just retribution for my sin were inflicted on Jesus instead. That's how much You love me — that You sent Him into the world, not to condemn me, but to save me.

I am horror-struck by the enormity of the price He paid to rescue me. Part of me recoils and wants to refuse His gift and to say, 'No, I can't accept it. It's too unjust.' Yet that would be to trivialise Your love. It would be ungrateful to turn aside and not acknowledge His sacrifice on my behalf.

Father, grant me the grace to put the past behind me, to turn my back on the ways and patterns, habits and attitudes of sin. Father, may Your Holy Spirit set fire to the house of my past so that it is burned to the ground and I cannot go back to it.

Father, forgive me for all those ways and patterns habits and attitudes that separated me from You and from the world You love.

I step down from the throne of my life. I give it to Jesus of Nazareth, Your beloved Son, Your Chosen One in whom You delight. And I say, 'Jesus is Lord.' I commit myself to listening to Him and I surrender into Your keeping all of my mind, heart, soul and strength so that I will learn to love You more each day.

I ask that this prayer be granted, in and through the name of Jesus and the saving power of His cross.

Amen

Acknowledgments & Attributions

Photo and Arts Credits

Cover and page 4 — Andrew_Howe /istockphoto | Description: Bright coloured kingfisher diving down off branch

Page 1 — coldblade/istockphoto | Description: Kingfisher on the hunt, Israel

Page 7 — leprechaun-fotolia/dollarphotoclub | Description: Banias Stream near Caesarea Philippi

Page 8 — D-Keine/istockphoto | Description: Monk wearing traditional clothes with sword

Page 11 — Adinfinum/istockphoto | Description: Tower of David arch with narcissus

Page 12 — Photo Credit: denisgo/ istockphoto | Description: Jewish holiday background with old book and landscape concept

Page 13 — Frank Ramspott/istockphoto | Description: 3D Render of a Topographic Map of Israel, Middle East; ackleyroadphotos/istockphoto | Description: White dove in flight

Page 14 — HisWondrousWorks/istockphoto | Description: Miracle of Yahshua

Page 15 — aviron/canstockphoto | Description: Old Roman gold coin 50 AD from Judea used as a tax for the Jewish temple known as MAHATSIT HASHEKEL (Half Shekel)

Page 16 — LUMO – The gospels for the visual age/lightstock | Description: Jesus calls His first disciples

Page 17 — odyphoto/istockphoto | Description: Architectural antiquities in natural reservation of Hermon river (Banyas) – Cult center of the God Pan, north of Israel

Page 18 — undefined undefined/istockphoto | Description: Ancient Spartan warrior in the helm and spear in hand is fighting; artfotodima/canstockphoto | Description: Beautiful Egyptian woman like Cleopatra on golden background

Page 18 — frantic00/istockphoto | Description: Goat herd leader with huge horns unusual

Page 19 — D-Keine/istockphoto | Description: Man who looks like Jesus Christ

Page 20 — D-Keine/istockphoto | Description: Knight looking through cross hole

Page 22 — Anke/canstockphoto | Description: Apostle Peter knowing Jesus

Page 25 — Creative_Hearts/canstockphoto | Description: Angelic female face transforming into a sinister occult goat-horned figure against a background of mysterious alchemy symbols

Page 26 — PavlovskiJenya/istockphoto | Description: Complete grains close-up. Against the sky with the sun. The idea of a rich harvest.

Page 29 — Alex_Vinci/istockphoto | Description: Israel, Palestine, a shepherd

Page 31 — avian75/istockphoto | Description: Wild ibex standing on the edge of a cliff over the Dead Sea

Page 32 — panaramka/canstockphoto | Description: Narcissus Valley

Page 34 — kostab/istockphoto | Description: At the bottom of a mountain, Israel

Page 35 — Genevieve Arthy | Description of painting: 'Walking on Water'

Page 36/37 — Alex Veresovich/Dollarphotoclub | Description: Blooming white narcissus

Page 39 — boryak/istockphoto | Description: Mount Hermon is a mountain cluster in the Anti-Lebanon mountain range. The southern slopes of Mount Hermon extend to the Israeli portion of the Golan Heights

Page 40 — Rndmst/Dreamstime.com | Description: Common crane birds in Agamon Hula bird refuge, with Mount Hermon in the background. Hula Valley, Israel

Page 42/43 — lucidwaters/canstockphoto | Description: Almond orchard and Mt Hermon in Spring, Israel

Page 44 — ipopba/istockphoto | Description: worship concept

Page 45 — Yellow1972/Dreamstime.com | Description: Snow Landscape on Hermon Mountain

Page 46 — Lorado /istockphoto | Description: Beautiful blonde sword-wielding warrior female in Game of Thrones style covered in henna tattoos; Daniel MG Gray/lightstock | Description: male lion

Page 47 — Kharchenko_irina7/istockphoto | Description: Worshipping the great old sacred stone, kneeling in the middle of a frozen forest, covered with frost; Juanmonimo/istockphoto | Description: Muslim woman praying stock photo

Page 48 — vasakna/istockphoto | Description: Angel at the hole of heaven

Page 49 — pixunfertig/Pixabay | Description: Winged lion

Page 50 — lermannika/canstockphoto | Description: Yellow vented Bulbul

Page 52 — Genevieve Arthy | Description of painting: 'Transfiguration'

Page 54 — studioalef/istockphoto | Description: Two lions at waterhole

Page 57 — amite/istockphoto | Description: Mount Hermon, Golan Heights, Israel

Page 59 — jgroup/istockphoto | Description: The Great Feast; D-Keine /istockphoto | Description: Jesus Christ in sunshine

Page 60 — YoriHirokawa/istockphoto | Description: Milky Way and stars reflected on the surface of the water at Uyuni. Standing in the middle of galaxy; Tom Askew/lightstock | Description: Man entering the temple doors

Page 63 — impr2003/istockphoto | Description: Pied Kingfisher stock photo

Page 65 — Pearl/lightstock | Description: Jesus extending His hand with an invitation to follow Him.

Page 70 — magann/lightstock | Description: Red light around earth; ackleyroadphotos/istockphoto | Description: White dove in flight

Design, including endpapers and floral iconography: Beckon Creative | beckoncreative.biz

Feather graphics by Elena Dorosh and Natalka Dmitrova | Creative Market

Bible Versions

Scripture quotations used in colour (red or blue) throughout the text are taken from the Holy Bible, New International Version®, NIV®. Copyright © 1973, 1978, 1984, 2011 by Biblica, Inc.™ Used by permission of Zondervan. All rights reserved worldwide. www.zondervan.com The "NIV" and "New International Version" are trademarks registered in the United States Patent and Trademark Office by Biblica, Inc™.

Scripture quotations marked BSB are taken from the The Holy Bible, Berean Study Bible, BSB Copyright ©2016 by Bible Hub Used by Permission. All Rights Reserved Worldwide.

Scripture quotations marked CJB are taken from the Complete Jewish Bible by David H. Stern. Copyright © 1998. All rights reserved. Used by permission of Messianic Jewish Publishers, 6120

Scripture quotations marked ESV are taken from the ESV® Bible (The Holy Bible, English Standard Version®), copyright © 2001 by Crossway, a publishing ministry of Good News Publishers. Used by permission. All rights reserved.

Scripture quotations marked GNT are from the Good News Translation in Today's English Version- Second Edition Copyright © 1992 by American Bible Society. Used by Permission.

Scripture quotations marked HCSB®, are taken from the Holman Christian Standard Bible®, Copyright © 1999, 2000, 2002, 2003, 2009 by Holman Bible Publishers. Used by permission. HCSB® is a federally registered trademark of Holman Bible Publishers.

Scripture quotations marked LEB are taken from the *Lexham English Bible*. Copyright 2012 Logos Bible Software. Lexham is a registered trademark of Logos Bible Software.

Scripture quotations marked NAS are taken from the New American Standard Bible®, Copyright © 1960, 1962, 1963, 1968, 1971, 1972, 1973, 1975, 1977, 1995 by The Lockman Foundation. Used by permission. (www.Lockman.org)

© Anne Hamilton 2020

Published by Armour Books

P. O. Box 492, Corinda QLD 4075 AUSTRALIA

ISBN: 978-1-925380-23-1

All rights reserved. No part of this publication may be reproduced, stored in, or introduced into a retrieval system, or transmitted, in any form, or by any means (electronic, mechanical, photocopying, recording or otherwise) without the prior written permission of the publisher.

A catalogue record for this book is available from the National Library of Australia

The world is charged with the grandeur of God.
It will flame out, like shining from shook foil;
It gathers to a greatness, like the ooze of oil
Crushed. Why do men then now not reck his rod?
Generations have trod, have trod, have trod;
And all is seared with trade;
bleared, smeared with toil;
And wears man's smudge
and shares man's smell: the soil
Is bare now, nor can foot feel, being shod.

And for all this, nature is never spent;
There lives the dearest freshness deep down things;
And though the last lights off the black West went
Oh, morning, at the brown brink eastward, springs —
Because the Holy Ghost over the bent
World broods with warm breast
and with ah! bright wings.

Gerard Manley Hopkins

www.ingramcontent.com/pod-product-compliance
Lightning Source LLC
Chambersburg PA
CBHW042252100526
44587CB00002B/114